D0856413

GRAPHIC HEROES OF THE AMERICAN REVOLUTION

PAUL REVERE AND HIS
MIDNIGHT RIDE

BY GARY JEFFREY
ILLUSTRATED BY JAMES FIELD

Gareth Stevens
Publishing

Please visit our website, www.garethstevens.com.
For a free color catalog of all our high-quality books,
call toll free 1-800-542-2595 or fax 1-877-542-2596.

Library of Congress Cataloging-in-Publication Data

Jeffrey, Gary.
Paul Revere and his midnight ride / Gary Jeffrey.
p. cm. — (Graphic heroes of the American Revolution)
Includes index.
ISBN 978-1-4339-6020-8 (pbk.)
ISBN 978-1-4339-6021-5 (6-pack)
ISBN 978-1-4339-6019-2 (library binding)
1. Revere, Paul, 1735-1818—Juvenile literature. 2. Massachusetts—
History—Revolution, 1775-1783—Juvenile literature. 3. United States—
History—Revolution, 1775-1783—Juvenile literature. 4. Statesmen—
Massachusetts—Biography—Juvenile literature. 5. Massachusetts—
Biography—Juvenile literature. I. Title.
F69.R43J44 2011
974.4'03092—dc22
[B]
2010050925

First Edition

Published in 2012 by
Gareth Stevens Publishing
111 East 14th Street, Suite 349
New York, NY 10003

Copyright © 2012 David West Books

Designed by David West Books
Editor: Ronne Randall

Photo credits:
p4, kirinqueen; p22, Daderot

Printed in China

CPSIA compliance information: Batch #DS11GS: For further information contact Gareth Stevens, New York, New York at 1-800-542-2595.

CONTENTS

After the Boston Tea Party in 1773, Britain tried to limit the freedoms of the people of Massachusetts. The colonists fought back by setting up their own government, called the First Continental Congress. The British were no longer in control.

The First Continental Congress

Minutemen were colonial militia, ready for action at a moment's notice.

Samuel Adams was a thorn in the side of the British Crown.

READY FOR DUTY

During the Congress, the patriot leader Samuel Adams got all the colonies to agree to stop buying British goods. In the fall of 1774, Adams also helped set up the first teams of minutemen. Colonists who were against British rule called themselves the Sons of Liberty.

THE WATCHFUL SILVERSMITH

Paul Revere was a successful craftsman and the leading member of a group called the Mechanics, a network of thirty men who spied on the British troops in Boston. During the spring of 1775, he delivered messages to patriot leaders like Samuel Adams and John Hancock. It was now too dangerous for them to be in Boston.

Paul Revere was a 41-year-old family man when he made his famous ride.

This view of Boston Harbor in 1774 shows the British fleet. It was engraved by Paul Revere.

THREATENED ACTION

Joseph Warren was the acting patriot leader in Boston. Revere helped him draw up plans for action if the British took over. On April 16, 1775, the Mechanics got warning that the British were preparing their landing boats…

PAUL REVERE AND HIS
MIDNIGHT RIDE

APRIL 18, 1775, 10:00 P.M. THE BOSTON HOME OF JOSEPH WARREN.

...YOU MUST GO AND WARN THEM, MR. REVERE!

BRITISH SOLDIERS, KNOWN AS THE KING'S REGULARS, WERE ABOUT TO INVADE MASSACHUSETTS FROM BOSTON BY BOAT.

THEIR TARGETS WERE THOUGHT TO BE THE PATRIOT LEADERS SAMUEL ADAMS AND JOHN HANCOCK.

AT 11:30 P.M., HE REACHED MEDFORD.

WAKE UP THE CAPTAIN. THEY'RE COMING!

THE REGULARS ARE COMING ACROSS BY BOAT!

WITH THE CAPTAIN OF THE MINUTEMEN ALERTED, REVERE RODE ON.

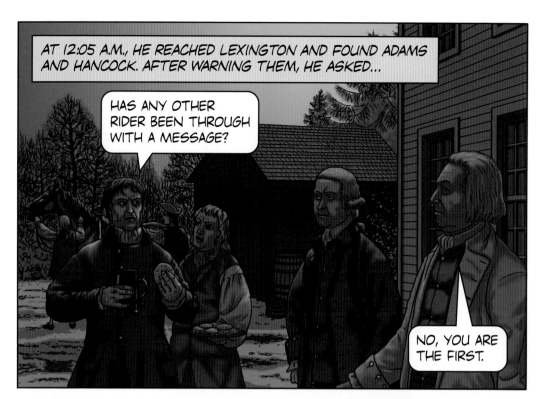

AT 12:05 A.M., HE REACHED LEXINGTON AND FOUND ADAMS AND HANCOCK. AFTER WARNING THEM, HE ASKED...

HAS ANY OTHER RIDER BEEN THROUGH WITH A MESSAGE?

NO, YOU ARE THE FIRST.

AT 12:30 A.M., THE OTHER RIDER ARRIVED. HE WAS A SHOEMAKER NAMED WILLIAM DAWES.

DAWES, I'M GOING TO RIDE ON TO CONCORD AND WARN THE TOWN.

I'M WITH YOU!

THE MILITIA HAD STORED SUPPLIES AT CONCORD.

REVERE AND DAWES MADE HASTE.

LOOK OUT BEHIND – A RIDER APPROACHES!

IT WAS A PATRIOT CALLED PRESCOTT WHO WAS TRAVELING HOME.

I WILL COME WITH YOU. I KNOW THIS ROAD WELL!

SIX REDCOATS AWAITED HIM..

...OH, NO!

A BRITISH MAJOR QUESTIONED REVERE.

WHAT TIME DID YOU LEAVE BOSTON?

AT TEN O'CLOCK, AND YOU'D BETTER WATCH OUT. THERE'LL BE FIVE HUNDRED PATRIOT SOLDIERS WAITING FOR YOU AT LEXINGTON!

THE GUNSHOTS MADE THE BRITISH OFFICERS NERVOUS. AFTER SWAPPING REVERE'S HORSE FOR A TIRED HORSE, THEY LEFT.

COME ON, YOU *NAG*, LET'S GO INTO LEXINGTON.

WHEN HE REACHED THE TOWN, HE MET JOHN LOWELL, JOHN HANCOCK'S SECRETARY.

MR. REVERE, A TRUNK FILLED WITH IMPORTANT PAPERS HAS BEEN LEFT IN THE TAVERN.

I WILL HELP YOU FETCH IT!

AS REVERE LOOKED BACK, THE AMERICANS AND BRITISH OPENED FIRE ON EACH OTHER.

BANG!

BANG!

BANG!

BANG!

BANG!

BANG!

BANG!

BANG!

REVERE CARRIED THE TRUNK TO SAFETY, THE FIRST SHOTS OF THE REVOLUTIONARY WAR RINGING IN HIS EARS.

THE END

There were many riders that night spreading the word all over Massachusetts. This helped the Battles of Lexington and Concord become patriot victories and sparked off the War of Independence. It would be eight long years before victory was achieved. During the war, Paul Revere helped set up a gunpowder mill and became a lieutenant colonel.

After the war, Revere returned to metalworking. His company cast the first bell made in Boston. He died in 1818.

A REVERED FIGURE

For many years after his death, Revere's ride was known only as a local folktale in Massachusetts. Then, in 1861, Henry Wadsworth Longfellow published a poem about Revere. The poem proved very popular, and over the years, the ride has become a powerful symbol of American liberty.

PAUL REVE

A statue of Paul Revere stands in Boston's North End.

GLOSSARY

Boston Tea Party An important event when a group of colonists, known as the Sons of Liberty, stood up against unfair British taxes. They boarded ships and threw the tea into the Boston Harbor.

colonist A person who settles in or sets up a new colony.

fleet A group of warships that operate together.

haste Speed or urgency.

invade To enter by force in order to conquer.

militia A group or army of ordinary citizens, who are not professional soldiers.

minutemen A group of militia who are ready to fight on a minute's notice.

nag An old, worn-out horse.

patriot A person who feels loyalty toward their country, and supports and defends it.

redcoat A British soldier who wore a red uniform jacket.

sentry A guard, often a soldier who prevents people entering a place without permission.

tavern An inn for travelers to sleep in.

INDEX

A
Adams, Samuel, 4–7, 11

B
Battles of Lexington and Concord, 22
Boston, 5, 6, 7, 16, 22
Boston Tea Party, 4

C
Charles River, 8
Charlestown, 7–9
Concord, 11, 13

D
Dawes, William, 11–12, 15

F
First Continental Congress, 4

H
Hancock, John, 5–7, 11, 18

K
King's Regulars, 6, 10, 19

L
Lexington, 7, 11, 16–18, 20
Lowell, John, 18–19

M
Massachusetts, 4, 6, 22
Mechanics, the, 5
militia, 4, 11, 20
minutemen, 4, 10

P
patriot, 6, 12, 16, 22
Prescott, 12, 15

R
redcoats, 7, 9, 13–14, 16, 20
Revolutionary War, 21

S
Sons of Liberty, 4

W
War of Independence, 22
Warren, Joseph, 5–6